Introduction

A picture is worth a thousand words. Teachers of literature have long been skeptical of the maxim, and with good reason. Where would classic adventure tales like *Moby Dick* and *Treasure Island* be without vivid descriptions and exciting dialogue? And what of favorites such as *Little Women* and *The Wizard of Oz*—books that rely on lyrical language and elegant prose to tell a story?

At first glance, graphic novels—which themselves can take the form of visual adaptations of these classics—can strike lovers of literature as problematic. They bear resemblance to comic books, with their vertical and horizontal frames bursting with colorful pictures, and speech bubbles and thought clouds hovering above characters' heads. Teachers may wonder why they would want to incorporate graphic novels into their classrooms. But it's difficult to argue with the popularity of this genre among young readers. According to *School Library Journal,* U.S. readers spent approximately $330 million on graphic novels and comics in 2006. Among them, librarians spent about 10 percent, or $33 million, on this genre.

Michael R. Lavin, a reference and collection development librarian for over 25 years, writes on Brodart.com that "graphic novels motivate reluctant readers, encourage reading of all types, and stimulate literary exploration." He points out studies indicating that young people who read graphic novels frequently seek out other types of books for pleasure reading, as well—sometimes even more so than their peers who don't read graphic novels. This newest generation of readers exists in a highly-visual landscape. Television, movies, magazines, newspapers, books, and computer monitors surround young people, offering a nonstop feast of imagery. Graphic novels pair vibrant illustrations with thought-provoking prose to draw young readers into a story.

While it's tempting to dismiss this genre as replete with superheroes and one-dimensional villains, graphic novels offer complex plots and relevant themes. Michele Gorman, teen services manager at the Public Library of Charlotte & Mecklenburg County in Charlotte, North Carolina, writes that "graphic novels are now addressing important personal and social issues like the power of imagination, being true to one's self, the benefits of teamwork, and how to cope with divorce and bullying." She also notes that teachers transitioning children from picture books to text-only books find graphic novels an effective and engaging bridge.

Using Graphic Novels in the Classroom focuses on literary graphic novels, both classic and contemporary. It invites students to review the basic elements of literature, which are similar whether a story is told in straight prose or pictures, and asks them to apply this knowledge to a book which you've selected for classroom reading. Through instruction in literary analysis, readers learn that graphic novels—at first glance colorful comic books—contain skillful plot construction, thoughtfully-drawn characters and conflicts, and richly-evocative language.

We hope that this book will deeply engage young readers in the pages of literary graphic novels, and inspire them to explore books further through art, script writing, and performance. With equal attention paid to illustration and writing, students may well come to the conclusion that where literature is concerned, a picture may not be worth a thousand words, but it can greatly enhance them.

How to Use This Book

Using Graphic Novels in the Classroom is divided into three sections. The first allows students to explore the unique genre of graphic novels. They study structure, art, syntax, symbolism, figurative language, design, and vocabulary.

The second part of this book asks students to analyze a specific graphic novel. This may be a book that you are reading together as a class. Your students may choose to complete the exercises in this section of the book as a group, or individually. Alternatively, you may ask each student to select a graphic novel with your approval and complete the exercises on his or her own. You may also put students into groups of three or four and ask each group to select and analyze a chosen graphic novel.

The third part of this book asks students to write and illustrate a graphic short story. It offers guidelines on brainstorming words and images, charting a plot, and planning the setting for visual scenes in the story. Bound with a cover and "About the Author" page, it will make a colorful final project with which to demonstrate students' new understanding of graphic novels.

Each lesson in *Using Graphic Novels in the Classroom*, Grades 4–8 meets one or more of the following standards, which are used with permission from McREL (Copyright 2007, McREL, Mid-continent Research for Education and Learning. Telephone: 303/337-0990. Website: **www.mcrel.org**)

Standards and Benchmarks	Page Number(s)
Uses a variety of prewriting strategies; drafts and revises writing.	35-37, 39, 42-45
Writes expository compositions, narrative accounts, and biographical sketches.	32, 35-37, 42, 43
Writes in response to literature; answers discussion questions and summarizes book.	all
Uses descriptive language that clarifies and enhances ideas (e.g., establishes tone and mood, uses figurative language, uses sensory images and comparisons).	14, 19, 20, 26, 27, 34-47
Uses grammatical and mechanical conventions in written compositions.	all
Gathers and uses information for research.	21, 29, 35
Uses the general skills and strategies of the reading process.	all
Understands character development, literary devices, point of view, cause and effect, and theme.	15, 16, 22, 23, 30-33
Uses listening and speaking strategies for different purposes.	39
Uses viewing skills and strategies to understand and interpret visual media.	6, 10, 11, 15, 16, 30, 38
Demonstrates competence in writing scripts and acting; designs and produces productions.	39-41, 44
Understands the historical perspective.	29
Knows some of the effects of various visual structures (e.g., design elements such as line, color, shape; principles such as repetition, rhythm, balance) and functions of art.	8, 9, 42, 43
Knows different subjects, themes, and symbols (through context, value, and aesthetics) which convey intended meaning in artworks.	9-12, 28, 42, 43
Understands how time and place influence visual, spatial, or temporal characteristics that give meaning or function to a work of art.	17, 18, 42, 43

Editor
Sara Connolly

Illustrator
Kevin Barnes

Cover Artist
Kevin Barnes

Editor in Chief
Ina Massler Levin, M.A.

Creative Director
Karen J. Goldfluss, M.S. Ed.

Art Coordinator
Renée Christine Yates

Imaging
Rosa C. See

Publisher

Mary D. Smith, M.S. Ed.

Author

Melissa Hart, M.F.A

Teacher Created Resources, Inc.
6421 Industry Way
Westminster, CA 92683
www.teachercreated.com

ISBN: 978-1-4206-2363-5

© 2010 Teacher Created Resources, Inc.
Made in U.S.A.

Table of Contents

What Is a Graphic Novel?

A novel is a book-length work of fiction. It is rich with character and setting. It has dialogue and plot. It offers vivid language and sensory details. It also includes conflict and resolution. Sometimes, a novel even includes illustrations.

Graphic novels <u>always</u> include illustrations. Pictures presented in a framework on each page tell the story. Graphic novels may be middle-grade stories that take place in the present. They may be adaptations of classic stories, which become shorter, but keep the basic plot. They can explore myths and legends. They can examine famous figures from history. They can even tell fairy tales. Regardless of the subject matter, graphic novels include characters, setting, dialogue, descriptive language, and a plot that offers conflict and resolution.

The first widely-known graphic novel is titled *Maus*. It was written by Art Spiegelman. He told the story of his father's experience during the Holocaust. In *Maus*, he use animals instead of people to tell the story. Like *Maus*, today's graphic novels are book-length stories told in a frame-by-frame format on each page.

Graphic Novels Versus Comic Books

How is a graphic novel different from a comic book? The first comic books were published in the early 1900s. They included stories about superheroes such as Batman and Superman. Later comic books told stories about teenagers, such as Archie and Friends. Detective comic books like Dick Tracy were also popular. Most comic books offer serial stories—that is, each book contains part of a story, but you must read the next book to find out what happens.

Graphic novels usually offer a stand-alone piece of literature—that is, a full story. The word "literature" refers to a piece that is skillfully written. The graphic novels you'll be reading for *Using Graphic Novels in the Classroom* represent literature. Whether they are historical, classic, or contemporary, the writing in these books is well crafted.

Think you understand the difference between graphic novels and comic books? Take the true-false quiz below to find out.

1. A short version of Moby Dick with pictures is a comic book.   True   False
2. A graphic novel can be one chapter of a longer story.   True   False
3. Superman is a comic book character.   True   False
4. The writing in graphic novels is often well crafted and skillful.   True   False
5. Comic books are often short versions of classic literature.   True   False
6. Graphic novels and comic strips use pictures to help tell a story.   True   False

Graphic Novel Vocabulary

Just as baseball players talk about *strikes* and *slides into home*, and actors talk about *running lines* and *playing to a full house,* graphic novelists have their own specialized vocabulary.

Directions: Study the vocabulary and examples below. Then, complete the sentences.

---

panel: a box or other shape that serves as a frame for a particular scene.

gutter: the space between panels on a page.

splash page: a single-panel page at the front of some graphic novels with vivid colors and exciting action that makes readers want to enter into the story.

inking: coloring in the black-and-white lines of a frame with paint, crayons, colored pencils, etc.

lettering: adding text to graphic novel pages, either by hand or on the computer.

bleed: An image that stretches up to, or even past, the edge of a graphic novel page.

crosshatch: drawing lines close to one another on an object to create shadows.

speed lines: short lines that run parallel to each other to suggest quick movements.

silhouette: a shadow outline of a person, animal, or object without clear details.

---

1. A giant dinosaur foot that steps off the panel and into the bottom margin of a page is called a

   _____ .

2. A graphic artist who wants to show a runner in a race would use

   _____ .

3. The process of adding color to black-and-white drawings in a panel is called

   _____ .

4. Graphic novelists draw characters and objects inside a

   _____ .

5. A graphic artist who wants to show the shadow cast by an oak tree on a field might ink the field with this type of line— _____ .

6. An author who writes words on each panel of a page is doing the

   _____ .

7. If a graphic artist didn't want readers to recognize a mysterious stranger right away, he or she might first show the person as a _____ .

8. The first page of a graphic novel, drawn as one exciting scene in a single panel, is called a

   _____ .

9. The thin or thick line between each panel is called a _____ .

Parts of Literature

Literature includes several parts, whether the story is classic or contemporary. Below, review the following parts of a novel before you study graphic novels.

Characterization—A novel has characters. These may be people, animals, or objects such as trees and rocks. Round characters are those who are complicated—they have different wants and needs. Like real people, they have both good and bad traits. Flat characters are described more simply. They are usually all good, or all bad. In a graphic novel, as in a traditional novel, you will see both round and flat characters.

Dialogue—Characters talk in graphic novels. This is called *dialogue*. Just as different people talk in different ways, characters in graphic novels each have their own way of talking. Some speak in complete sentences. Some use slang. You can learn a lot about a character by studying the way he or she speaks.

Plot—Every novel has a plot. Plot includes the *rising action*, the *climax*, and the *falling action*. The climax is the high point of the story. Rising action leads up to that high point, while falling action tells what happens after the climax of the novel.

Conflict—Every novel relies on conflict. *Conflict* is a problem between two or more characters. It can also be a problem that the character has with himself or herself. Conflict is what keeps us reading a novel. It creates tension and keeps us interested in the story. We want to know how characters will resolve their conflicts, and how they will grow and change because of these conflicts.

Resolution—When characters solve a problem, they have resolution. By the end of most novels, readers understand how each character's problem has been solved.

Setting—This is the location in which the characters are located. Setting can mean the time of day and the season. It can mean the time of year, from an ancient era to the far-off future. Setting can be close-up, taking place in a character's bedroom or in a school yard. It can also be far away, taking place in one particular state, country, or even planet. Setting tells the reader where the characters in a novel are.

Theme—This refers to the main idea or ideas that guide a novel from beginning to end. One common theme is "there's no place like home." Another theme in many novels is that of the "hero's journey"—a hero in a novel must make a long and dangerous trip in order to get from one place to another. Other popular themes explore the difficulty of being a new kid in school, how learning a new skill is both challenging and rewarding, and why it's important to follow common-sense rules so that you don't get hurt.

Point of View—Who is telling the story? Is it one character, who refers to himself or herself as "I," and only knows what's going on in his or her brain? Or, is it a narrator who knows everything about each character? Point of view may switch in a novel. Sometimes, stories are told from various points of view, in different characters' voices. Other times, just one character tells a story. And sometimes, the narrator tells the story.

Symbols, Colors, Balloons, and Boxes

Graphic novels use symbols, colors, balloons, and boxes to help tell a story. **Symbols** are objects that represent something else. For instance, a snake in a graphic novel can symbolize danger. An owl might be a symbol of wisdom.

Study the frame below. To the right, describe what each symbol might mean:

1. heart _____

2. eyelashes _____

3. mountain _____

4. dog _____

5. alarm clock _____

6. sweat drops _____

Colors can also be symbols. Certain colors make us think of certain things. Here is a list of what colors may symbolize in a graphic novel:

purple: royalty or magic   **blue:** tranquility

red: danger or excitement   **white:** innocence or mystery

yellow: warning or happiness   **black:** mystery

green: the environment or money   **pink:** femininity

orange: attention! Look at me!

Balloons and **boxes** in graphic novels let you know who is talking, and who is narrating the story.

> To be or not to be—that is the question

A **balloon** in a graphic novel indicates speech. The character's words appear inside the balloon.

A **burst** shows speech that is anxious, surprised, excited, or angry.

WOW!

Often, a character's thoughts appear in a **cloud** above his or her head.

> Pretty silly question, if you ask me.

A **box** in a graphic novel shows narration. The narrator tells the story within small boxes in the frames on each page.

> And so Hamlet moved on to the question of what he would have for dinner that night.

Symbols, Colors, Balloons, and Boxes *(cont.)*

Think further about how graphic novelists and artists use visual symbols, as well as colors, balloons, and boxes.

Directions: Fill in the chart to show what each object in a graphic novel might symbolize.

Object	What it Symbolizes	Object	What it Symbolizes
☺		👍	
💡		$	
☘		☠	

Now, fill in the blanks to show your understanding of how graphic novelists and artists use color as symbols.

a. An artist who wants to show that a house is haunted might color it _____.

b. A character who loves nature will likely wear clothing in shades of _____.

c. In a frame showing a dangerous battle, the artist will use the color _____.

d. A character who is young and innocent will probably wear the color _____.

e. If the artist wants to get our attention on one particular page of a novel, he or she will likely use the color _____.

f. When might a graphic novelist or artist make use of the color pink? _____

   _____

g. How might an artist use the color blue to show that a character is calm and happy?

   _____

   _____

Study the picture below. Draw one balloon, one burst, one thought cloud, and one box. Fill each in with writing to tell the story.

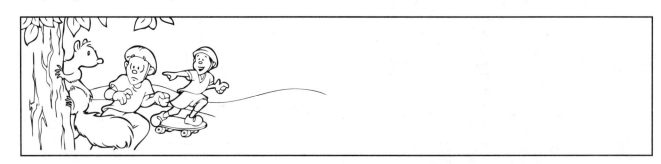

Character Emotions

On television or in movies, it's easy to show a character's emotions. In books, this is harder. Graphic novels allow readers to read a little about how a character is feeling. However, unlike a traditional novel, graphic novels don't leave room for pages and pages of description.

Graphic novels do allow us to study people's faces to know how they are feeling. They also give us clues based on body language. A character drawn with wide eyes, raised brows, and an open mouth is most likely scared or surprised. Someone with a down-turned mouth, lowered eyebrows, and slumped posture may be sad or angry.

Here is an example from *The Wizard of Oz*, during the scene in which Dorothy sees the Emerald City for the first time.

Emotion: Joy
Facial Expression: She is smiling, and her eyes are wide-open and excited.
Body Language: She is running toward the city. Her arms are outstretched. Her pigtails are streaming behind her.

Directions: Study the graphic frames below. Write the emotion you think the character is feeling. Describe the character's facial expression and body language.

	1. Emotion: 2. Facial Expression: 3. Body Language:
	1. Emotion: 2. Facial Expression: 3. Body Language:

Character Emotions *(cont.)*

Now it's your turn to draw how various characters are feeling.

Directions: Draw a character to illustrate the description listed at the bottom of each box. Pay close attention to facial expression and body language.

a girl who is afraid of bees	a bear who has discovered a picnic basket
a boy whose best friend just moved away	a cat surprised by a balloon popping

Tension and Suspense

In a full-length novel with no pictures, writers must create tension and suspense through exciting language. In a graphic novel, authors use spine-tingling images, as well as thrilling language, to show conflict and create exciting stories.

Sometimes, the artist will use jagged borders to build tension. Sometimes, he or she will use lightning bolts or close-ups of characters' faces looking tense, angry, or sad. Artists exaggerate the expression on characters' faces to ramp up the tension. They also use one-word dialogue balloons with exclamations like "No!," "Stop!," or "Help!"

Other times, graphic novelists and artists end the right-hand page with a *kicker*. A kicker in comic books may be the final frame of action on the very last page. In a kicker ending, the hero may be hanging from a cliff. He may be tied to a train track as a whistle sounds. She may be about to find out whether she has won a million dollars. But readers won't find out what happened until they buy the next comic book.

Most graphic novels, like traditional novels, do not have a kicker ending. By the time you finish the book, you know what has happened to the characters. But some authors use a kicker on the bottom last frame of every two-page spread. This makes readers want to turn the page to find out what happens. How do they create tension and suspense in the final frame?

Sometimes, graphic novelists and illustrators use humor.

Sometimes, they use a terrifying scene.

Other times, they use a mysterious picture.

And still other times, they show a sad scene.

Tension and Suspense *(cont.)*

Directions: Choose from one of the following scenes. Then draw four frames that build tension and suspense. Your last frame should use a kicker that makes readers want to turn the page to find out what happens next.

Graphic Novel Scenes

- a detective goes into a haunted house because he or she has heard someone screaming

- a starving bear rounds a corner and spots a herd of elk

- two kids are about to find out why all the cats in the neighborhood have vanished

- an aspiring actor goes to look at the audition results posted in the school window

Movement and Sound

A car swerves to avoid hitting a lost dog. An Olympic athlete drops to the track and weeps with joy. A hurricane blows. A cell phone rings. A villain gnashes his teeth.

Movement and sound are easy to communicate on film. A novelist will sometimes spend half a page describing how somebody walks or talks so that readers can see the action. But graphic novelists use just a few words on a page if that page contains a great deal of action. Using too many words detracts from the movement and sound on a page and makes the layout too "busy."

How do graphic novelists and illustrators convey movement? In both human and animal characters, they show flexed body-limbs with clear muscle definition. Many artists have taken classes in anatomy so that they can accurately draw what a body looks like when it is running, leaping, tiptoeing, or dancing.

To convey movement of objects, an illustrator may show glass shards flying from a newly-broken window, comets shooting past a rocket ship as it blasts into space, or sharp, black lines jutting out from the scene of a crash or a fall.

Sometimes, the artist uses sound-words to emphasize movement. Frequently, these sound-words are examples of *onomatopoeia*—that is, words that sound like the actions they describe. They're often followed by an exclamation point . . . or two!!

Here are some classic examples of onomatopoeia from graphic novels:

slam!	the sound a door makes when it closes hard
pop!	the sound a balloon makes when someone pokes it with a pin
boom!	the sound of an explosion
clackety-clack	the sound fingers make on a computer keyboard
screech!	the sound of a car as it brakes suddenly to a stop
sssss!	the sound of a snake, or of air leaking out of a tire
zzzzz	the sound of someone snoring

Now, think of three more examples of onomatopoeia. Write them and what they describe on the chart below.

Onomatopoeia Word	What It Describes

Perspective

Perspective refers to how a scene is shown—from close-up or faraway. It can also refer to *point of view*. It tells readers who is narrating a story or who is observing an action.

Graphic novels use several techniques to show perspective. The first technique is the **wide-angle**. A wide-angle gives readers a sense of where the scene is taking place. The frame might show the bottom of the Grand Canyon, the inside of someone's living room, or a galaxy. Often, the characters are very small in a wide-angle frame, to give a sense of a big space. However, there may still be dialogue in this type of scene.

The next form of perspective is the **long-shot**. This isn't as vast as a wide-angle frame, but it often contains at least two characters and most of their bodies. Readers can still see surrounding details such as rocks, furniture, or stars, but they don't see them as clearly. They do, however, see clothing and hair details much more clearly than they would in a wide-angle frame.

The next technique is the **close-up**. A frame that uses a close-up might choose to focus on a character's head as he or she speaks. But words aren't necessarily shown. A close-up can convey characters' sorrow by showing tears on their cheeks. It can show a character's anger by showing a furrowed brow and clenched teeth. It can let readers know that a character is happy by showing a wide smile and shining eyes.

An **extreme close-up** focuses on a very small part of a scene. A frame that shows only a golden cup overturned on a table might imply that the liquid inside contained poison. A frame that shows just a woman's hand with a large diamond ring on one finger might emphasize her wealth or the idea that she's just gotten engaged. And an extreme close-up of sheriff's gold star might remind readers of a particular character's authority.

Perspective *(cont.)*

Directions: Now it's your turn. Below, describe what type of perspective you would choose for each scene given, following the example below. Choose between *wide-angle, long-shot, close-up,* and *extreme-close up.*

Scene: A sixth-grade student falls, trying to pick apples from a backyard tree. (Example)

Perspective	Description
close-up	I would show a girl's face as she lies on the grass with one bruised apple beside her. Her mouth is crooked with pain, and tears well up in her eyes.

Scene: A diver discovers buried treasure in a ship under the ocean.

Perspective	Description

Scene: A child looks up to see a seagull flying off with a hamburger.

Perspective	Description

Scene: A soldier waves a flag in the midst of a battle.

Perspective	Description

Scene: Three aliens look at Earth through the window of their spaceship.

Perspective	Description

Conveying Time

Time can mean many things in a graphic novel. It might mean the day of the week. It could mean morning, afternoon, evening, or midnight. It can mean winter, spring, summer, or fall. It might mean the Stone Age, the 1800s, today, or the year 2099. It could even mean an hour, a minute, or a second before the school bell rings.

How do graphic novelists and artists show time, and the passing of time, in graphic novels? On the previous two pages, you learned about perspective. Often, graphic novelists rely on perspective in a frame to give readers information about time. Here are some examples:

To show morning, an artist might draw a wide-angle frame of the sun just peeping up above the horizon line.

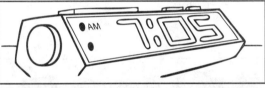

To show time in hours, minutes, and seconds, an artist might show an extreme close-up of an alarm clock.

To show midnight, the artist may draw a long-shot of a crescent moon high up in a black sky.

To show winter, the artist might show a close-up of a character in mittens, hat, and scarf, with chattering teeth and icicles hanging from his moustache.

To show a prehistoric era, the artist will likely draw a wide-angle frame showing ancient trees, along with dinosaurs.

To show a contemporary era, the artist has to pay attention to what people are wearing, eating, and driving. He or she has to be aware of today's technology, as well.

There are many ways to show the passage of time in a graphic novel. The easiest is to draw one frame with the words "one day later," "Monday morning," or "the year 2009," for example. But the artist might also draw characters getting older, with new wrinkles, grey hair, and hunched body posture. The artist might also show a change in seasons by drawing bare tree limbs that have leaves in a later frame, or characters bundled up against snow and then wearing shorts and tank tops on another page of the novel.

Conveying Time *(cont.)*

Directions: Study each frame on the novel page below. Write the time frame on the line below each frame.

Time of day?

_____

Season?

_____

Month?

_____

Day of week?

_____

Hour?

_____

Time of day?

_____

Key Concepts in Literature

Novels, whether they are traditional or graphic, use several key concepts. Here are a few of the most popular, below, with descriptions of how they might apply to your chosen graphic novel.

Alliteration: This term refers to what happens when several words in a sentence begin with the same sound. For example, in Tom Sawyer, a graphic novelist might write, "On Tuesday, Tom talked and talked until he was tired out."

Deus ex Machina: This Latin term translates as "God in a machine." It refers to a novel which ends with someone or something unexpectedly saving the main characters.

Flashback: This is when the author tells a story, but pauses midway through to remind readers of something that occurred in the past. For example, halfway through a graphic novel version of *The Red Badge of Courage,* the author might include a frame that shows the main character as a child playing war with his friends.

Foreshadowing: This is when the author hints at what is going to happen long before it actually occurs. For example, the first frame of a graphic mythological novel might show Romulus and Remus ruling all of Rome as adults, but the next frames on several pages tell the story of how the boys were born and raised by a wolf.

Hyperbole: This is exaggeration. Authors use hyperbole to create drama or humor. For example, in a graphic novel version of "Rip van Winkle," Rip might wake up after twenty years to find that his beard is so long that he steps on it. This shows that he's been asleep for a very long time.

Irony: This term refers to a situation in which the outcome is not what readers expected. For example, in *Peter Pan,* you would not expect the ferocious Captain Hook to be deathly afraid of a crocodile. It is ironic that such a fierce man would be scared of a small animal.

Metaphor: When the author compares one thing to another, in order to help readers to understand it more clearly, he or she has crafted a metaphor. For instance, in the graphic novel version of *Little Women,* Jo might tell her sister Meg, "Your stylish friends remind me of a flock of nervous chickens."

Personification: This happens when the author gives human traits to a nonhuman creature or object. For example, in *The Wizard of Oz,* the Cowardly Lion, the Scarecrow, and the Tin Man are all examples of personification.

Simile: This is similar to a metaphor, but a simile uses the word "like" or "as" to make a more direct comparison between one thing and another. In *Treasure Island,* the main character might discover sacks of gold and say, "The coins shine like the sun."

Key Concepts in Literature *(cont.)*

Directions: Match the literary concepts below to the situation which best describes them.

1. metaphor

2. alliteration

3. irony

4. deus ex machina

5. simile

6. hyperbole

7. foreshadowing

8. flashback

9. personification

a. In *Nancy Drew*, Nancy says that her best friend "has gone as pale as a ghost!"

b. In *Medea*, the main character thwarts death at the end of the story when the sun god sends down a chariot for her escape into the sky.

c. In *Little Women*, Amy says, "My nose is so large that birds can perch on it."

d. In *King Arthur and the Knights of the Round Table*, the author tells the story of Arthur as a boy, and shows a frame in which he dreams that he is a king.

e. In *Dracula*, the graphic novelist writes, "The vengeful vampire vanished into a violet night."

f. In *Black Beauty*, the author shows the horse pulling a heavy carriage, then adds a frame in which Black Beauty remembers being a happy foal on a peaceful farm.

g. In *Robin Hood*, the main character's very tall sidekick is named "Little John."

h. In *Call of the Wild*, the dogs talk among themselves about how they don't like to pull the sled.

i. In *The Wizard of Oz*, Dorothy says, "The city's glow puts me in mind of a giant emerald."

Vocabulary in Graphic Novels

The next section of this book invites you to explore a graphic novel chosen by you or by your teacher. Read the novel before completing this section. Write down the name of the novel you have selected:

_____   by _____

  novel name   author's name

Just as in traditional novels, graphic novels offer new vocabulary. Learning what unfamiliar words mean will enhance your enjoyment of a novel.

Directions: Begin by looking through your chosen graphic novel and writing down unfamiliar words on the chart below. Using a dictionary, write down the definition of each vocabulary word.

Vocabulary Word	Definition

Characterization

Characterization refers to how an author creates and develops characters. Specific traits help readers to understand them. For instance, a character may be funny, kind, and prone to envy. Another character may be physically strong, but easily scared and very quiet. Usually, characters show more than one trait.

Early in this book, you learned about round characters and flat characters. Round characters are those who show many different emotions. They are complex, just like you. They change and grow by the end of the novel. For instance, a middle-school student who loves math but cheats one time on an exam and then feels horrible is an example of a round character.

Flat characters are simple. They may only show one emotion. Sometimes, they show no growth or change by the end of a novel. For example, a bully who is always mean and never shows kindness throughout a book is a flat character.

Directions: Study the example below. Write down four characters from the graphic novel that you have chosen to study. Then list three of their strongest character traits. Finally, note whether you think each character is round or flat.

Character	Three Traits	Round or Flat?
Donnie Dragonowitz	always combing his hair great sense of humor afraid of spiders	round

Character	Three Traits	Round or Flat?

Characterization *(cont.)*

Whether a character is round or flat, he or she wants something. The math-lover wants a good grade on a test and later, wants to feel like a good person despite having cheated. The bully may want to feel stronger than someone else.

Directions: Draw a picture of yourself in the frame below. In a balloon, write three things you want in a complete sentence.

Directions: Look at your list of characters from the previous page. Choose three "round" characters. Think about what they want. In the frames below, draw a picture of each character. In a balloon, write down what the character wants in one complete sentence. In some cases, your characters will want more than one thing. It's okay to write as many as you can think of!

Finally, on the lines below, explain how each character above grows and changes by the end of the book. See the example for ideas.

Example: <u>At the beginning of the book, Dorothy is tired of living on a farm in Kansas with her</u> <u>grandparents. By the end of the book, she realizes she loves her life, and that there really is "no place</u> <u>like home."</u>

Character 1:_____

_____

Character 2:_____

_____

Character 3:_____

_____

Conflict

You want your mother to buy chocolate ice cream at the store, but your sister wants strawberry. Your parents want to move to a new city, but you want to stay where you are. These are conflicts.

Conflict is an important part of any novel. No one wants to read a story in which everything is perfect. When a character has a problem, readers want to know how it is solved. This keeps them reading!

Here are some classic conflicts in literature:

Literature	Conflict
Black Beauty	Black Beauty suffers at the hands of cruel owners who beat her.
Treasure Island	Jim Hawkins is afraid of the pirates, and he witnesses a murder.
Tom Sawyer	Tom gets engaged to Becky, but she rejects him when she finds out he has been engaged before.

There are several types of conflict in a novel. Here are the most common:

In *character versus self*, a character shows internal conflict. For example, in the novel *Peter Pan*, Wendy knows she should stay in bed, but she wants to learn to fly.

In *character versus character*, a character has a problem with another character. In *Peter Pan*, Captain Hook doesn't like the crocodile because it ate his hand.

In *character versus society*, a character has a problem with what society expects of him or her. Peter Pan doesn't want to become an adult, even though society says that everyone must grow up.

In *character versus environment*, a character has a problem with a place. For example, in *Peter Pan*, the pirates strand Tiger Lily on Marooners' Rock, where the sea threatens to drown her.

Directions: Choose one character from your graphic novel. Below, write a short essay that describes this character's conflicts. Explain at least two conflicts and note which types they are. Refer to the list above for help.

_____

_____

_____

_____

Conflict *(cont.)*

On the previous page, you learned about four different types of conflict in novels. Can you find all four in your graphic novel?

Directions: Read through your chosen graphic novel. Identify one example of each type of conflict: *character versus self, character versus character, character versus society,* and *character versus environment.*

In each of the four frames below, draw a picture that shows the type of conflict described. Write dialogue in balloons, bursts, or thought clouds to explain the conflict.

Character Versus Self	**Character Versus Character**
Character Versus Society	**Character Versus Environment**

Dialogue and Narration

Graphic novels tell a story through pictures and words. The words appear in three forms—monologue, dialogue, and narration.

monologue = a long speech by a single character.

dialogue = a conversation between at least two characters.

narration = a recital of the events in a story.

Many traditional novels have between 80,000 and 100,000 words. Graphic novels often tell a story in just a few thousand words. Graphic novelists have to get good at saying a lot through very little writing.

Directions: Study the writing below. The left-hand column contains writing from a traditional novel. The right-hand column shows writing from a graphic novel.

Excerpt from a Traditional Novel	Excerpt from a Graphic Novel
When she realized what her father had packed for lunch, Cindy was so grateful. She decided to share her slice of birthday cake with the new girl in her class. But she ate her favorite egg salad sandwich on wheat bread all herself.	
Jon searched and searched, but he could not find his dog. He walked up to Mr. Green's door and knocked softly. "I'm sorry to bother you," he said to the elderly man, "but have you seen a Collie?" Mr. Green shook his head. "No, but I'll be on the lookout for your dog," he said. Mr. Green felt sad. Years ago, he had lost his beloved terrier.	
The exhausted elephant dragged her body to the watering hole. "I barely have the strength to drink," she murmured. "What a long, long trip I've had from the zoo back to my home in Africa." The other elephants looked at the iron bracelet around her leg. They thought she smelled funny, like popcorn. They felt a little afraid of their newly-returned sister.	

Dialogue and Narration *(cont.)*

Directions: Now it's your turn. Below, study the writing from the traditional novel on the left side of the chart. On the right side, draw a picture and write just a few words that convey the same ideas as the longer piece of writing.

Excerpt from a Traditional Novel	Excerpt from a Graphic Novel
Lyra wasn't sure what to do. Ms. Smith expected her to care for her cat, but Lyra had lost the key to her house. If she didn't break a window, Ms. Smith's cat might starve to death. "If I break a window," she thought, "I might get hurt. And I'll have to pay for the damage. What should I do?"	
Simon and Jacob had planned a surprise party for their best friend, Mouse. But Simon's little sister told Mouse about the party. "I wish she wasn't my sister," Simon told Jacob. Mouse smiled. "It's okay," he said. "I don't really like surprises. It's more fun knowing I'm going to have a party next week!"	

Now, study the graphic novel selection on the left side of the chart below. On the right side, write out the action you see, along with dialogue and/or monologue.

Excerpt from a Graphic Novel	Excerpt from a Traditional Novel
WHOMP!	

Point of View

Point of view explains who narrates a story. It can also tell who observes a particular scene at any given moment. Here are four common points of view in a novel:

First-person limited—This narrator refers to himself or herself as "I." This person only knows what is happening in his or her own brain.

First-person omniscient—Omniscient means "knowing all." This narrator refers to himself or herself as "I," but he or she knows what every other character is thinking, too!

You can usually tell when a narrator is speaking from a first-person point of view. The graphic artist features images of this narrator more than other characters. This first person narrator is often drawn in great detail, while minor characters are less detailed or may be merely silhouettes. The first-person narrator is often the only character in a panel, with close-ups on his or her face.

Third-person limited—This narrator follows one character around and knows what is going on in only that person's head. The narrator refers to that character by name or as "he" or "she."

Graphic artists drawing a third-person limited point of view will focus on one character more than the others. The character will appear often in panels, frequently with close-ups on his or her face. The narration will be in a box.

Third-person omniscient—This narrator follows all of the characters in a story around and knows what everyone is thinking. The narrator refers to each character by name or as "he" and "she."

Graphic artists drawing this point of view will give equal space to each character. There may be close-ups of each character in a panel, at some point in the book. There may also frequently be long-shots of the entire group of characters.

Directions: Choose one page from the graphic novel you are reading. Sketch one panel in the box below. Beside it, note which point of view is shown in the panel. Explain how you know which point of view is being shown.

Point of View: _____

Explanation: _____

_____

_____

_____

Now, on a separate piece of paper, draw the same panel from a different perspective. If the panel from your book is drawn from a third-person perspective, choose one character and draw the panel from a first-person perspective instead. If the panel is drawn from a first-person perspective, draw the scene from a third-person narrator's perspective. You may choose to either a limited or omniscient point-of-view.

Historical Background

Often, history informs a novel's setting. A novel may be set in the prehistoric era. It may be set in colonial New England or in France during World War II. A novel may be set in the future as well. Learning about the time in which your graphic novel is set will help to deepen your understanding of the book.

In what year does your graphic novel take place? Write it here: _____

In what location does your graphic novel take place? Write it here: _____

Directions: Using books, encyclopedias, and the Internet, research the historical time period and place in which your novel is set. Answer the questions below to the best of your ability:

1. Who had power over the land (was it a king, a queen, a president, a dictator, etc.?)

   _____

2. What conflicts (war, poverty, slavery, illness, etc.) occurred?

   _____

3. What were the primary modes of transportation? _____

4. What technology (the printing press, the cotton gin, television, cellular phones) did people use?

   _____

5. What did people eat? _____

6. What type of music did they listen to? _____

7. What did these people do for entertainment? _____

8. What did these people do for work? _____

Now, on a separate sheet of paper, draw a graphic panel to explain the history of the era (real or imagined) in which your graphic novel is set. See the example below for ideas.

©Teacher Created Resources, Inc.   29   #2363 Using Graphic Novels in the Classroom

Plot Pyramid

Plot structure refers to the action in a novel. It is often charted on a pyramid, made up of the parts below.

Directions: Study the five parts of the plot. Then read the sample that illustrates the plot pyramid structure.

The first part of the novel is the **introduction**. It introduces characters and setting. It may tell readers what the main character wants. It may also introduce one or more conflicts suffered by a main character or characters.

The second part of the novel introduces the **rising action**. It explores at least one problem experienced by a main character or characters. It explains why these characters cannot yet get what they want.

The **climax** is the most exciting part of the novel. It's a turning point for a main character or characters. The conflict is most powerful during the climax of a story. Readers aren't sure whether the characters will actually get what they want.

Near the end of the book, there is **falling action**. The characters begin to settle down. They may still have problems, but they are beginning to be resolved.

Resolution appears at the end of the novel, in which some characters get what they want, and some don't.

Plot Chart

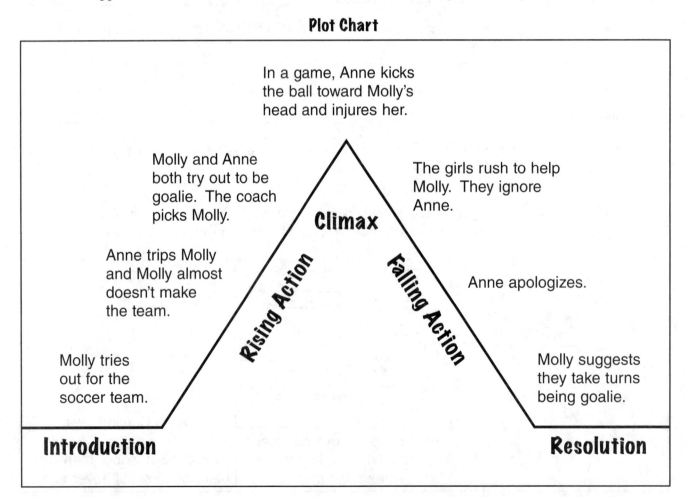

Graphic Novel Themes

The *theme of a novel* is its main idea. The writer hopes to make a point about society or the environment or about human or animal nature. All novels, including graphic novels, contain a theme. Here are some sample themes from literature:

- It is important to be true to yourself and resist peer pressure.
- People who are dishonest will eventually get caught in their lies.
- If you are ambitious and you work hard, you will achieve your goals.
- Loyal friends will not abandon each other in times of conflict.

Often, a graphic novel contains more than one theme. An author may strongly explore one theme, but examine other themes as well.

Directions: Think about the graphic novel you have chosen to read. Write down as many themes as you can think of from the book. Then, circle the strongest theme. At the bottom of the panel below, write the theme. Then, make up a scene that best illustrates this novel's theme. Sketch it in the panel, and then outline and color it. Feel free to use balloons, bursts, or boxes for dialogue or narration in your scene.

Persuasion Chart

Usually, the main character in a novel wants something to happen or to stop happening. He or she hopes to persuade other characters to believe the same thing. For example, a character might hope to persuade an entire country that we should save polar bears. Another character might hope to persuade her friends that her family is rich, when actually, they have very little money.

Persuasive people know that they must state their beliefs clearly, and then support them with facts and examples. They also use emotional appeals to persuade people. Some characters are good at this, and they inspire others to believe as they do.

Directions: Think about a character from your chosen graphic novel, and what he or she wants to happen or stop happening. Study the example below. Then, fill out the chart below to show how this character tries to persuade others to feel or think the same thing.

Character: ____Jonas____ (Example)

What He Wants	Facts	Emotional Appeals
Jonas wants to persuade people to save polar bears.	Polar bears are in danger of becoming extinct. Polar bears maintain a healthy food chain by preventing overpopulation of seals.	Jonas carries a stuffed polar bear around with him. He shows photos of starving polar bears and melting glaciers.

Character: _____

What He/She Wants	Facts	Emotional Appeals

Cause and Effect

Every story shows cause and effect. A character earns a "D" on a test, and because of this, he decides that he doesn't like science. Another character finds a stray kitten, and it inspires her to start a cat shelter.

cause = stray kitten   effect = cat shelter

Directions: Think about how cause and effect appears in the graphic novel you have been studying. Choose three examples of cause and effect and illustrate them in the boxes below. Explain each cause and effect below the boxes in the space given.

Cause = _____   Effect = _____

Cause = _____   Effect = _____

Cause = _____   Effect = _____

Sensory Details

As you read your graphic novel of choice, can you feel the cold breeze as the characters walk across a field at midnight? Can you smell the beautiful red roses that one character offers another? Can you taste the hot chocolate that a character drinks, and can you hear the ghostly howl of a coyote as you read?

Graphic novelists rely on sensory details to bring their story to life for readers. *Sensory details* are those that explore how something smells, feels, tastes, sounds, and looks. Most people rely mainly on their sight to give them information about an object or scene, but the other senses are extremely important, as well, as anyone who has ever smelled freshly-baked chocolate chip cookies will tell you!

Directions: Read through your graphic novel, paying close attention to the sensory details that the writer and artist have put into it. Look at the example below, then fill out the chart below to note which details in your chosen novel appeal to your five senses.

Taste	Smell	Touch	Sound	Sight
Mr. Munson eats sweet strawberries in one scene.	Sachi smells a foul odor from the sewer in one panel.	A stray kitten rubs against Sachi. She says it's soft.	Mr. Munson hears the long wail of a foghorn.	Sachi spots a tiny pink butterfly on a leaf in the park.

Taste	Smell	Touch	Sound	Sight

Graphic Author Biography

Think about the person who wrote and possibly illustrated the graphic novel that you have been studying. Did he or she like to read or draw as a child? Did he or she have brothers and sisters? Where did this person grow up? Did he or she go to college? How did this person come to write this particular graphic novel? And is he or she working on another graphic novel at the moment?

Directions: Using encyclopedias and biographies from your library, and/or the Internet, research the author and/or illustrator of your chosen graphic novel. If your novel is an adaptation of a classic such as *Tom Sawyer* or *Twenty Thousand Leagues Under the Sea*, research the original author. You will be able to find plenty of information on classic authors both in books and on the Internet. If your novel is more recent, note that the author likely has a website. You can visit it to learn all about him or her.

In your research, take written notes on the following:

- When and where was this person born?
- Where did this person grow up?
- What type of family did this person have (One or two parents? Brothers? Sisters? Grandparents?)
- Did this person have any pets as he or she was growing up?
- What interests did this person have as a child? Did he or she enjoy reading and drawing?
- What books did this person love to read as he or she was growing up?
- Did this person attend college? If so, where?
- What made this person want to be an author?
- How did this person get the idea for the novel you've been studying?
- Does this person say anything in particular about this novel in the articles you have researched? If so, write down a quote or two.
- Is this person working on a new graphic novel?
- Can you write a fan letter to this person? If so, where can you send it?

Now that you have done research on the author of your graphic novel, locate a drawing, painting, or photo of this person. You will need it for the final part of this assignment. Sketch the author in the space to the right.

Finally, tell this author's biographical story in graphic novel form. First, you'll need to determine the important parts of this person's life. You'll also need to think about the important people (and possibly animals) in this person's life. You'll want to think about perspective and point of view, setting, and how each frame of this biography will look.

On the next page, answer the questions to begin planning your graphic author biography. Then, on a piece of paper, draw frames that illustrate the different parts of this person's life. In balloons and bursts, give this author dialogue. You can also add narration in boxes. Feel free to include other characters such as siblings, parents, friends, or spouses in the biography, as well.

Graphic Author Biography *(cont.)*

Directions: Answer the questions below before you complete your graphic author biography.

Prewriting Questions

1. What are the most important parts of this author's life? Note them below:

   A. _____

   B. _____

   C. _____

   D. _____

   E. _____

   F. _____

   G. _____

2. What quote or quotes from this author would you like to include in your biography? Write the quote(s) here:

   _____

   _____

   _____

3. What main characters (people and/or animals) from this author's life should appear in your biography? Note them here:

   A. _____

   B. _____

   C. _____

   D. _____

4. Do you want to tell this author's story from a first-person point of view, or from a third-person point of view?

   _____

Pre-drawing Questions

5. Look at the author photo you've found. What physical details do you need to put into your illustrations of this person (curly hair, glasses, bushy eyebrows, baseball cap, etc.)? Note the details below:

   A. _____

   B. _____

   C. _____

   D. _____

6. Think about setting. What places have been most important to this author? Her office? The ocean? A classroom? Paris? Note these important settings below:

   A. _____

   B. _____

   C. _____

7. What graphic techniques will you use to tell this author's story? Balloons? Bursts? Bleeds? Note them below:

   A. _____

   B. _____

   C. _____

Review of a Graphic Novel

When you finished reading your graphic novel, did you love it or dislike it? Did you enjoy one character but despise another? Did you think the dialogue was natural or forced?

Most books get reviewed by newspapers, magazines, Internet sites, and journals. The reviewer tries to be very honest about what he or she thought of the book. This assignment asks you to write a book review of your graphic novel.

Directions: First, get familiar with what a book review looks like. Go to your local library or type the titles below into the Internet to read a few book reviews from the following magazines:

The Horn Book   **Bookhooks.com**
Through the Looking Glass   **Teenreads.com**

Notice that many book reviews offer a brief summary of the novel's plot, as well as a sense of what the reviewer thought of the book.

> King Arthur and the Knights of the Round Table
> a review by Anna McDaniels
>
> This graphic novel was about the adventures of King Arthur and the kingdom of Camelot. My favorite character was King Arthur, because he was brave. I did not like Lancelot because he was disloyal to the king. Sometimes I skipped over some of the dialogue to get to the battle scenes. I was most interested in the action scenes, and the pictures were really colorful and exciting. I liked it when all the knights were joined together at the round table, but I was disappointed when Guinevere and Lancelot betrayed the king's trust. The story was really good, and I would like to read more graphic novels like this one.

Now, answer the following before you write your review:

1. Which characters in this graphic novel did you like? Why?

   _____

2. Which characters did you dislike? Why?

   _____

3. Did the dialogue grab your attention, or did you find yourself skipping over parts of it? Explain below:

   _____

4. Did the plot of this graphic novel keep you interested, or were parts of it boring? Explain below:

   _____

5. What parts of this graphic novel did you like the best?

   _____

6. What parts of this graphic novel did you like the least?

   _____

Now, write a review of your graphic novel on a separate page. Draw pictures to illustrate it.

Dramatizing Literature

When you dramatize a piece of literature, you create a performance taken from a story or poem. The next section of this book asks you to choose a favorite scene from your graphic novel and turn it into a play.

You'll need to work in a group to write a script, develop characters, decide on sound and lighting effects, and come up with costumes. After you brainstorm and rehearse your scene, you will give a performance for your class!

Directions: Get into a group of three or four students. Choose a scene from your graphic novel to turn into a short play. Study the roles below. In your group, decide who will take on each role. Note that each person can take on more than one role. For instance, the props person may also be an actor.

Director—This person is responsible for helping the actors to rehearse the script. He or she watches the actors closely and gives advice for how to show emotion and build tension. The director may ask the actors to speak more clearly, to show more or less emotion, or to move in a certain way.

Stage Manager—This person is responsible for sound and lighting. He or she may play music and other sound effects like shoes clomping up stairs, a baseball shattering a window, or an owl hooting in the night. The stage manager is also responsible for dimming or turning up the lights on the performance.

Costumer—This person helps the actors to gather together their costumes for the performance. He or she may research the time period so that the actors' costumes are correct. He or she will even make sketches to show how each actor should look during a scene.

Props Person—This person is in charge of the props (short for properties) that appear on stage. He or she thinks about the setting and then decides on the objects that should be on stage. This person may be responsible for gathering objects such as furniture, books, and toys. He or she may also create pretend settings with cardboard trees, castles, or spaceships, for example!

Actor—This person assumes the role of a character from the script. He or she is responsible for becoming this character on stage. This person studies the character from the novel and the script and decides what emotions to convey. He or she may work together with the director, the stage manager, the costumer, and the props person to develop a complex, believable character.

Below, note which person in your group will take on each role. Write down the main characters from the scene you have chosen, and decide who will act out each role.

director	
stage manager	
costumer	
props person	
character 1 (name: _____)	
character 2 (name: _____)	
character 3 (name: _____)	
character 4 (name: _____)	

Writing a Script

Books often become movies or plays. Think of *Harry Potter, Because of Winn-Dixie,* and *Hoot.*

Sometimes, the author of the book also writes the script for the movie or play. Other times, someone else writes the script. Most scripts contain the following:

Stage directions to tell actors where and when they should enter and exit the stage. They also tell people where to stand while they are on stage.

Example: Maria enters stage left and moves toward the dog.

Character notes to tell actors what they should be doing in a particular scene, and what emotions they should show while they say certain lines.

Example: Jonas (pounding on the table and yelling): I don't want to go to summer camp!

Lighting and sound cues to tell the stage manager (the person in charge of lights and sound) when to make lights dim or bright and when to add or fade away sound).

Example: Sound of doorbell. Sachi runs off stage. *Fade lights and music.*

The next few pages ask you to write a script version of one section of your graphic novel and then act it out for your class. You'll think about body language and facial expression. You'll build emotion and create tension. All of these will bring this graphic novel to life for your audience.

Directions: Study the sample script below. Then, write a script for the scene you've chosen from your graphic novel. Decide on costumes and props, as well.

Scene: The school playground. Four kids (Rob, Li, Carlos, and Janell) play Capture the Flag on a sunny day while the song "You are My Sunshine" plays.

Fade out song.

Janell: (stops running and says with excitement) What a beautiful day! I feel like nothing bad can happen on such a day.

Rob: (trips over his shoelace and falls into the sand) Speak for yourself, Janell. I just got sand in my mouth.

Carlos: (stands on top of slide and waves "flag" in victory) Janell's right, Rob. It's a perfect day.

Li: (looking off stage right) Did anyone hear someone scream?

A long scream echoes from stage right. All of the kids look at one another.

Everyone together: Someone's in trouble!

Rob, Li, and Carlos run off stage right. Janell stands alone. Fade in "You Are My Sunshine."

Janell: (looking sadly down at her shoes) I guess I was wrong.

Janell runs off stage. Fade out music.

Body Language and Facial Expression

You have learned how artists who draw pictures for graphic novels pay close attention to the body language of characters to show their emotions. You have also learned that they show how characters are feeling by drawing particular expressions on their face.

Actors must use their own body language and facial expressions to show emotions. In a graphic novel, a character who is feeling happy may stand tall and smile. In a play, the character needs to show even more emotion. He or she may bounce happily across the stage or sing a cheerful song. The character may pick an imaginary flower or speak in a high-pitched, energetic voice.

Directions: In your group, discuss each character in your script. Talk about how the actor portraying that character should look. What body language should that actor show? What expressions should appear on his or her face? Look at the example below, and then fill out the chart.

Character	Body Language	Facial Expression
Marisol Fuentes	Marisol is afraid of the dark. Her shoulders are hunched and she is trembling. She holds a blanket tight around her.	Her eyes are wide, and her eyebrows are raised. Her mouth is downturned, and her teeth are chattering.

Character	Body Language	Facial Expression

Conveying Tone and Building Tension

Tone refers to the emotion of a scene. Is it cheerful or scary? Is it sorrowful or hectic?

The actors' body language and facial expression convey tone on stage. They also help to build tension. There are other ways to show mood and tension, too, through sound and movement.

For a scary, tense scene, the stage director might choose to use intense music that makes the audience feel anxious. He or she might record and play the sound of breaking glass or a car screeching to a halt or ambulance sirens.

For a cheerful scene, the stage director might play a happy song that makes the audience want to sing along. He or she might record and play the sound of birds singing, the music of an ice-cream truck, or children laughing in the distance.

To build tension, the actors might begin to pace nervously across the stage. They may start to talk louder or even yell. They might argue with one another. But tension doesn't have to be frightening. To convey positive tension, they might hop up and down in eager anticipation. They might begin to talk loudly, but happily. They might hug each other and trade joyful looks.

Directions: Get into your dramatization group. What is the tone of your scene? Write it here:

_____

What is the climax of your scene? Describe it here in one sentence:_____

_____

Brainstorm how to convey emotion and build tension in your scene by filling out the chart below:

What music will you use to convey tone?	
What music will you use to convey tension?	
What sound effects will you use to convey tone?	
What sound effects will you use to convey tension?	
What will the actors do to convey tone?	
What will the actors do to convey tension?	

Brainstorming

The next section of this book will guide you through writing a graphic short story of your own. You'll brainstorm ideas and outline a plot. You'll develop characters and setting. You'll also create dialogue and draw pictures to illustrate your story.

Directions: Answer the following questions below to generate ideas for your graphic short story.

1. Who will be the main character(s) in your graphic short story? Write each character's name, age, and a brief description of him/her in the space below.

   _____

   _____

   _____

2. Who will be the minor character(s) in your graphic short story? Write each character's name, age, and a brief description of him/her in the space below.

   _____

   _____

   _____

3. Where will your short story be set? Below, note details including the day, month, and year, as well as the locations in which your story is set.

   _____

   _____

4. What is the main conflict in your short story? Describe it below.

   _____

   _____

5. What is the climax (the high point) of your short story? Describe it below.

   _____

   _____

   _____

6. How will the conflict in your short story be resolved? Describe the resolution below.

   _____

   _____

   _____

Graphic Short Story Plot

Many novelists—both traditional and graphic—plot out the story before they write it. They chart the plot on the computer or on a big piece of paper so that they know what happens to the characters at every point in the story.

Directions: Refer to the plot chart on page 30. Then, plot your own story in the boxes on the graphic chart below.

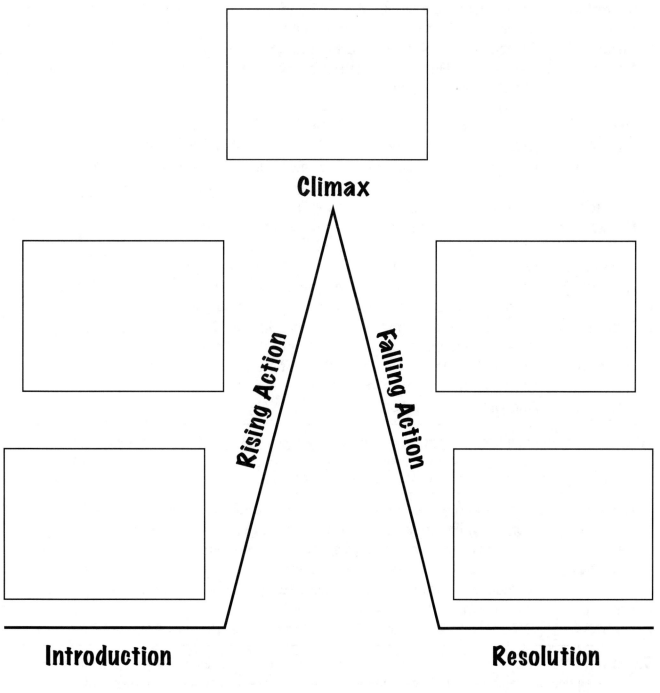

Climax

Rising Action

Falling Action

Introduction

Resolution

Writing a Script and Editing

Many graphic novelists write a script for their story before transferring dialogue and narration to the balloons and bursts on each page. After they've written a script, they may edit so that the words fit in each frame. They also carefully check their spelling, punctuation, and grammar before transferring the words from the script onto the graphic novel page.

Here is an example of a sample script from a graphic short story.

Narration:	Once, there were two brothers who loved to ride bicycles.
Damien:	Someday, I'm going to ride in the Olympics.
Nate:	Someday, I'm going to bicycle across the country.
Narration:	Damien and Nate rode together every day after school. Sometimes, they bicycled for two hours!
Damien:	Whoo. I'm tired.
Nate:	C'mon—let's pedal up just one more mountain.
Narration:	Nate was a strong rider. He could bicycle all day.
Damien:	I'm faster on my bike, but after a few hours, I'm exhausted.
Nate:	That's why you're perfect for the Olympics!
Narration:	But one day, Damien hit a rock and fell.
Damien:	I broke my leg and couldn't compete in the Olympic trials.
Nate:	That's okay. I'll compete for you. Whoopee!
Damien:	Oh, wow! He took first place. My brother is going to the Olympics!
Narration:	Damien tried to be cheerful, but he felt sad. As his leg healed, he rode his bike long, slow distances and thought about his Olympic dream.
Damien:	I'm not a fast rider anymore, but look! I rode 100 miles today!
Nate:	I wish I could bicycle across the country, but I'm too busy now.
Narration:	The brothers looked at each other. Then they had an idea.
Nate:	I'll ride in the Olympics for Damien.
Damien:	And I'll bicycle across the country for Nate!

After a writer has completed a script, he or she decides which lines will appear in speech balloons, which will appear in thought clouds, which will be in bursts, and which will be in boxes. The writer may note this right on the script. See the sample, below.

Narration:	Once, there were two brothers who loved to ride bicycles.	← *box*
Damien:	Someday, I'm going to ride in the Olympics.	← *speech balloon*
Nate:	Someday, I'm going to bicycle across the country.	← *speech balloon*
Narration:	Damien and Nate rode together every day after school. Sometimes, they bicycled for two hours!	← *box*
Damien:	Whoo. I'm tired.	← *burst*
Nate:	C'mon—let's pedal up just one more mountain.	← *speech balloon*

Directions: Now it's your turn. On a separate sheet of paper, write a script for your graphic short story. Then decide which lines will be in boxes, and which lines will appear in speech balloons, thought clouds, and bursts.

Character Study

In previous sections of this book, you learned the importance of developing complex characters in a graphic novel. You also learned that each character wants something, and that main characters show at least one type of conflict in a graphic novel. You have already described the characters in your graphic short story briefly. This assignment asks you to examine at least one character more in depth.

Directions: Fill out the biography page below to develop the main character in your graphic short story. If you prefer, you may copy the page on a separate sheet of paper and fill one out for each character in your short story.

Character Biography

1. Character's Full Name _____

2. Age_____

3. Species _____

4. Eye Color_____

5. Hair Color _____

6. Height/Weight _____

7. Favorite Foods _____

Draw a picture of your character in this box.

8. Favorite Sport _____

9. Hobbies _____

10. Biggest Fear _____

11. Best Friend _____

12. What this character wants more than anything _____

_____

13. What is standing in the way of this character's greatest want _____

_____

14. Other important details about this character _____

_____

Setting the Scenes

You have learned about the importance of the setting in telling a story. Readers will want to know what day, month, and year it is in each scene. They will want to know if your story takes place in the morning, afternoon, or evening. They will want to see each scene in vivid detail. Remember that you will color your graphic short story, and recall that you can use individual colors as symbols.

See the sample setting below for ideas on how to plan out a scene.

- Use blue to symbolize calm day.

- Sand is brown, grey, white, and black.

- Main character lives in cave here.

Directions: Fill out the chart below and sketch in the squares provided to help you plan the scenes in your graphic short story. This space allows for four scenes, but you may copy the chart on a separate sheet of paper if you need more scenes for your story.

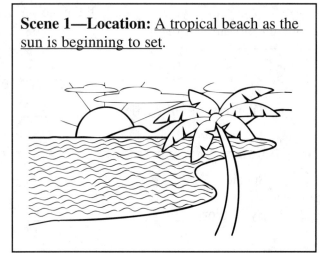

Scene 1—Location: A tropical beach as the sun is beginning to set.

Scene 1—Location: _____

_____

Scene 2—Location: _____

_____

Scene 3—Location: _____

_____

Scene 4—Location: _____

_____

Your Graphic Short Story

You've done the prewriting and pre-drawing strategies. You've gotten to know your characters, and you've set the scene and chosen colors. Now it's time to craft your graphic short story!

Materials:

- scratch paper, 8 ½" x 11"
- two-to-three sheets of 8 ½" x 11" cardstock, per person
- pencil
- three-hole punch
- metal brads
- crayons, colored pencils, or paints
- black fine-point pen
- ruler (optional)

Directions: Make a sketch of your graphic short story on scratch paper with a pencil. Make sure to draw all panels, as well as rough images and letters. This is called your layout. Then, punch holes in the left 11" side of your pieces of cardstock, one at a time. Place one piece of cardstock in front of you, with the holes to your left side. This side of the cardstock will be the cover of your graphic short story. Write the name of the story, the author's name, and then illustrate the cover to get readers interested in the story.

Flip your cover page over. This side will be the first page of your graphic short story. Divide the page into frames. With a pencil, draw the characters and words inside each frame. Color the objects within your frame. Then, trace over each penciled outline with a black fine-point pen.

Place the next piece of cardstock in front of you with the holes to your left. This will be the second page of your graphic short story. Repeat the steps for the first page of your short story.

Flip the second page over to the blank side. This is your "About the Author" page. Here, you will include an illustration of yourself, as well as a brief biography. Study the example to the right for ideas.

When all of the ink on your pages is dry, put your book together with metal brads. Alternatively, you may thread ribbon or string through the holes and tie it in bows or knots to bind your short story. Display the graphic short story in your classroom or school library for everyone to read and enjoy!

About the Author

Matt Mazorati grew up in Manhattan Beach, California. When he was two years old, he began to draw in the sand with a stick. Now, he draws all the time—even in math class.

He got the idea for this story when a frog jumped through his bedroom window and landed on his pillow.

Bonus Project: Now that you know how to write a book review, consider trading graphic short stories with another student. Read his or her story, and then write a review of it, noting what you liked best. Display the review next to the student's short story in your classroom or school library.

Bibliography

Books on How to Write a Graphic Novel

Chinn, Mike. *Writing and Illustrating the Graphic Novel.* (Barron's, 2004)

Eisner, Will. *Graphic Storytelling and Visual Narrative.* (Norton, 2008)

Gravett, Paul. *Graphic Novels: Everything You Need to Know.* (Collins, 2005)

Classic Literature in Graphic Novel Form for the 4–8 Classroom

Grahame, Kenneth. Adapted by Michel Plessix. *The Wind in the Willows.* (Papercutz, 2008)

Hall, M.C. and C. E. Richards. *King Arthur and the Knights of the Round Table* (retold). (Stone Arch, 2006)

London, Jack. *Call of the Wild.* (Puffin, 2006)

Sewell, Anna. Adapted by June Brigman and Roy Richardson. *Black Beauty.* (Puffin, 2005)

Shelley, Mary. Adapted by Gary Reed. *Frankenstein.* (Puffin, 2005)

Stevenson, Robert Louis. Adapted by Tim Hamilton. *Treasure Island: The Graphic Novel.* (Puffin, 2005)

Twain, Mark. *Graphic Classics: Mark Twain.* (Eureka, 2007)

Favorite Contemporary Graphic novels for the 6–8 Classroom

Colfer, Eoin. *Artemis Fowl.* (Hyperion, 2007)

Holm, Jennifer L., and Matthew. *The Babymouse* series. (Random House, publication dates vary)

Satrapi, Marjane. *Persepolis: The Story of a Childhood.* (Pantheon, 2004)

Siegel, Siena Cherson. *To Dance: A Ballerina's Graphic Novel.* (Aladdin, 2006)

Smith, Jeff. *The Bone* series. (Scholastic, publication date varies)

Tan, Shaun. *The Arrival.* (Arthur A. Levine, 2007)

Yang, Gene Luen. *American Born Chinese.* (First Second, 2006)

Books and Articles Designed to Increase Awareness of Graphic Novels

Carter, James Bucky. *Building Literary Connections with Graphic Novels: Page by Page, Panel by Panel.* (NCTE, 2007)

Gorman, Michele. "Graphic Novels Rule: The Latest and Greatest for Young Kids." *School Library Journal,* March 1, 2008.

Hart, Melissa. *Media Literacy: Grades 5, 6, 7–8.* (Teacher Created Resources, 2008)

Kist, William and David Bloome. *New Literacies in Action: Teaching and Learning in Multiple Media.* (Teachers College Press, 2004)

Answer Key

Page 5	Page 6		Page 9	Page 20	
1. F	1. bleed	6. lettering	**Chart:**	1. i	6. c
2. F	2. speed lines	7. silhouette	Accept all reasonable answers.	2. e	7. d
3. T	3. inking	8. splash page	a. black	3. g	8. f
4. T	4. panel	9. gutter	b. green	4. b	9. h
5. F	5. crosshatch		c. red	5. a	
6. T		**Page 8**	d. white		
	accept all reasonable answers.		e. orange		
			f. to show a character who is feminine		
			g. Accept all reasonable answers.		